Medea

Medea

By

Seneca

Translated by Ella Isabel Harris

Enhanced Media
2017

Medea by Seneca. Translated by Ella Isabel Harris. First published in 1899. This edition published 2017 by Enhanced Media. All rights reserved.

Enhanced Media Publishing
Los Angeles, CA.

First Printing: 2017.

ISBN-13: 978-1543231366

ISBN-10: 1543231365

Contents

Dramatis Personae 7

ACT I 8

ACT II 12

ACT III 21

ACT IV 31

ACT V 36

Dramatis Personae

Jason
Creon
Medea
Nurse
Messenger
Chorus of Corinthian Women.

Scene— Corinth.

ACT I

Medea [alone]. Ye gods of marriage;
Lucina, guardian of the genial bed;
Pallas, who taught the tamer of the seas
To steer the Argo; stormy ocean's lord;
Titan, dividing bright day to the world;
And thou three-formed Hecate, who dost shed
Thy conscious splendor on the hidden rites!
Ye by whom Jason plighted me his troth;
And ye Medea rather should invoke:
Chaos of night eternal; realm opposed
To the celestial powers; abandoned souls;
Queen of the dusky realm; Persephone
By better faith betrayed; you I invoke,
But with no happy voice. Approach, approach,
Avenging goddesses with snaky hair,
Holding in blood-stained hands your sulphurous torch!
Come now as horrible as when of yore
Ye stood beside my marriage-bed; bring death
To the new bride, and to the royal seed,
And Creon; worse for Jason I would ask—
Life! Let him roam in fear through unknown lands,
An exile, hated, poor, without a home;
A guest now too well known, let him, in vain,
Seek alien doors, and long for me, his wife!
And, yet a last revenge, let him beget
Sons like their father, daughters like their mother!
'Tis done; revenge is even now brought forth—
I have borne sons to Jason. I complain
Vainly, and cry aloud with useless words,
Why do I not attack mine enemies?
I will strike down the torches from their hands,
The light from heaven. Does the sun see this,

The author of our race, and still give light?
And, sitting in his chariot, does he still
Run through the accustomed spaces of the sky,
Nor turn again to seek his rising place,
And measure back the day? Give me the reins;
Father, let me in thy paternal car
Be borne aloft the winds, and let me curb
With glowing bridle those thy fiery steeds!
Burn Corinth; let the parted seas be joined!
This still remains—for me to carry up
The marriage torches to the bridal room,
And, after sacrificial prayers, to slay
The victims on their altars. Seek, my soul—
If thou still livest, or if aught endures
Of ancient vigor—seek to find revenge
Through thine own bowels; throw off woman's fears,
Intrench thyself in snowy Caucasus.
All impious deeds Phasis or Pontus saw,
Corinth shall see. Evils unknown and wild,
Hideous, frightful both to earth and heaven,
Disturb my soul,—wounds, and the scattered corpse,
And murder. I remember gentle deeds,
A maid did these; let heavier anguish come,
Since sterner crimes befit me now, a wife!
Gird thee with wrath, prepare thine utmost rage,
That fame of thy divorce may spread as far
As of thy marriage! Make no long delay.
How dost thou leave thy husband? As thou cam'st.
Homes crime built up, by crime must be dissolved.

Scene II

*Enter Chorus of Corinthian women, singing the marriage song of Jason and
Creusa.*

Chorus. Be present at the royal marriage feast,
Ye gods who sway the scepter of the deep,
And ye who hold dominion in the heavens;
With the glad people come, ye smiling gods!

First to the scepter-bearing thunderers
The white-backed bull shall stoop his lofty head;
The snowy heifer, knowing not the yoke,
Is due to fair Lucina; and to her
Who stays the bloody hand of Mars, and gives
To warring nations peace, who in her horn
Holds plenty, sacrifice a victim wild.
Thou who at lawful bridals dost preside,
Scattering darkness with thy happy hands,
Come hither with slow step, dizzy with wine,
Binding thy temples with a rosy crown.
Thou star that bringest in the day and night,
Slow-rising on the lover, ardently
For thy clear shining maids and matrons long.
In comeliness the virgin bride excels
The Athenian women, and the strong-limbed maids
Of Sparta's unwalled town, who on the top
Of high Taÿgetus try youthful sports;
Or those who in the clear Aonian stream,
Or in Alpheus' sacred waters bathe.
The child of the wild thunder, he who tames
And fits the yoke to tigers, is less fair
Than the Ausonian prince. The glorious god
Who moves the tripod, Dian's brother mild;
The skillful boxer Pollux; Castor, too,
Must yield the palm to Jason. O ye gods
Who dwell in heaven, ever may the bride
Surpass all women, he excel all men!
Before her beauty in the women's choir
The beauty of the other maids grows dim;
So with the sunrise pales the light of stars,
So when the moon with brightness not her own
Fills out her crescent horns, the Pleiads fade.
Her cheeks blush like white cloth 'neath Tyrian dyes,
Or as the shepherd sees the light of stars
Grow rosy with the dawn. O happy one,
Accustomed once to clasp unwillingly
A wife unloved and reckless, snatched away
From that dread Colchian marriage, take thy bride,
The Æolian virgin—'tis her father's will.
Bright offspring of the thyrsus-bearing god,

The time has come to light the torch of pine;
With fingers dripping wine put out the fires,
Sound the gay music of the marriage song,
Let the crowd pass their jests; 'tis only she
Who flies her home to wed a stranger guest,
Need steal away into the silent dark.

ACT II

Scene I

Medea, Nurse.

Medea. Alas, the wedding chorus strikes my ears;
Now let me die! I could not hitherto
Believe—can hardly yet believe such wrong.
And this is Jason's deed? Of father, home,
And kingdom reft, can he desert me now,
Alone and in a foreign land? Can he
Despise my worth who saw the flames and seas
By my art conquered? thinks, perchance, all crime
Exhausted! Tossed by every wave of doubt,
I am distracted, seeking some revenge.
Had he a brother's love—he has a bride;
Through her be thrust the steel! Is this enough?
If Grecian or barbarian cities know
Crime that this hand knows not, that crime be done!
Thy sins return to mind exhorting thee:
The far-famed treasure of a kingdom lost;
Thy little comrade, wicked maid, destroyed,
Torn limb from limb and scattered on the sea
An offering to his father; Pelias old
Killed in the boiling cauldron. I have shed
Blood often basely, but alas! alas!
'Twas not in wrath, unhappy love did all!
Had Jason any choice, by foreign law
And foreign power constrained? He could have bared
His breast to feel the sword. O bitter grief,
Speak milder, milder words. Let Jason live;
Mine as he was, if this be possible,
But, if not mine, still let him live secure,
To spare me still the memory of my gift!
The fault is Creon's; he abuses power

To annul our marriage, sever strongest ties,
And tear the children from their mother's breast;
Let Creon pay the penalty he owes.
I'll heap his home in ashes, the dark flame
Shall reach Malea's dreaded cape, where ships
Find passage only after long delay.

Nurse. Be silent, I implore thee, hide thy pain
Deep in thy bosom. He who quietly
Bears grievous wounds, with patience, and a mind
Unshaken, may find healing. Hidden wrath
Finds strength, when open hatred loses hope
Of vengeance.

Medea. Light is grief that hides itself,
And can take counsel. Great wrongs lie not hid.
I am resolved on action.

Nurse. Foster-child,
Restrain thy fury; hardly art thou safe
Though silent.

Medea. Fortune tramples on the meek,
But fears the brave.

Nurse. This is no place to show
That thou hast courage.

Medea. It can never be
That courage should be out of place.

Nurse. To thee,
In thy misfortune, hope points out no way.

Medea. The man who cannot hope despairs of naught.

Nurse. Colchis is far away, thy husband lost;
Of all thy riches nothing now remains.

Medea. Medea now remains! Here's land and sea,
Fire and sword, god and the thunderbolt.

Nurse. The king is to be feared.

Medea. I claim a king
For father.

Nurse. Hast thou then no fear of arms?

Medea. I, who saw warriors spring from earth?

Nurse. Thou'lt die!

Medea. I wish it.

Nurse. Flee!

Medea. Nay, I repent of flight.

Nurse. Thou art a mother.

Medea. And thou seest by whom.

Nurse. Wilt thou not fly?

Medea. I fly, but first revenge.

Nurse. Vengeance may follow thee.

Medea. I may, perchance,
Find means to hinder it.

Nurse. Restrain thyself
And cease to threaten madly; it is well
That thou adjust thyself to fortune's change.

Medea. My riches, not my spirit, fortune takes.
The hinge creaks,—who is this? Creon himself,
Swelling with Grecian pride.

Scene II

Creon with Attendants, Medea.

Creon. What, is Medea of the hated race
Of Colchian Æëtes, not yet gone?
Still she is plotting evil; well I know
Her guile, and well I know her cruel hand.
Whom does she spare, or whom let rest secure?
Verily I had thought to cut her off
With the swift sword, but Jason's prayers availed
To spare her life. She may go forth unharmed
If she will set our city free from fear.
Threatening and fierce, she seeks to speak with us;
Attendants, keep her off, bid her be still,
And let her learn at last, a king's commands
Must be obeyed. Go, haste, and take her hence.

Medea. What fault is punished by my banishment?

Creon. A woman, innocent, may ask, 'What fault?'

Medea. If thou wilt judge, examine.

Creon. Kings command.
Just or unjust, a king must be obeyed.

Medea. An unjust kingdom never long endures.

Creon. Go hence! Seek Colchis!

Medea. Willingly I go;
Let him who brought me hither take me hence.

Creon. Thy words come late, my edict has gone forth.

Medea. The man who judges, one side still unheard,
Were hardly a just judge, though he judge justly.

Creon. Pelias for listening to thee died, but speak,

I may find time to hear so good a plea.

Medea. How hard it is to calm a wrathful soul,
How he who takes the scepter in proud hands
Deems his own will sufficient, I have learned;
Have learned it in my father's royal house.
For though the sport of fortune, suppliant,
Banished, alone, forsaken, on all sides
Distressed, my father was a noble king.
I am descended from the glorious sun.
What lands the Phasis in its winding course
Bathes, or the Euxine touches where the sea
Is freshened by the water from the swamps,
Or where armed maiden cohorts try their skill
Beside Thermodon, all these lands are held
Within my father's kingdom, where I dwelt
Noble and happy and with princely power.
He whom kings seek, sought then to wed with me.
Swift, fickle fortune cast me headlong forth,
And gave me exile. Put thy trust in thrones—
Such trust as thou mayst put in what light chance
Flings here and there at will! Kings have one power,
A matchless honor time can never take:
To help the wretched, and to him who asks
To give a safe retreat. This I have brought
From Colchis, this at least I still can claim:
I saved the flower of Grecian chivalry,
Achaian chiefs, the offspring of the gods;
It is to me they owe their Orpheus
Whose singing melted rocks and drew the trees;
Castor and Pollux are my twofold gift;
Boreas' sons, and Lynceus whose sharp eye
Could pierce beyond the Euxine, are my gift,
And all the Argonauts. Of one alone,
The chief of chiefs, I do not speak; for him
Thou owest me naught; those have I saved for thee,
This one is mine. Rehearse, now, all my crime;
Accuse me; I confess; this is my fault—
I saved the Argo! Had I heard the voice
Of maiden modesty or filial love,
Greece and her leaders had regretted it,

And he, thy son-in-law, had fallen first
A victim to the fire-belching bull.
Let fortune trample on me as she will,
My hand has succored princes, I am glad!
Assign the recompense for these my deeds,
Condemn me if thou wilt, but tell the fault.
Creon, I own my guilt—guilt known to thee
When first, a suppliant, I touched thy knees,
And asked with outstretched hands protecting aid.
Again I ask a refuge, some poor spot
For misery to hide in; grant a place
Withdrawn, a safe asylum in thy realm,
If I must leave the city.

Creon. I am no prince who rules with cruel sway,
Or tramples on the wretched with proud foot.
Have I not shown this true by choosing him
To be my son-in-law who is a man
Exiled, without resource, in fear of foes?
One whom Acastus, king of Thessaly,
Seeks to destroy, that so he may avenge
A father weak with age, bowed down with years,
Whose limbs were torn asunder? That foul crime
His wicked sisters impiously dared
Tempted by thee; if thou wouldst say the deed
Was Jason's, he can prove his innocence;
No guiltless blood has stained him, and his hands
Touched not the sword, are yet unstained by thee.
Foul instigator of all evil deeds,
With woman's wantonness in daring aught,
And man's courageous heart—and void of shame,
Go, purge our kingdom; take thy deadly herbs,
Free us from fear; dwelling in other lands
Afar, invoke the gods.

Medea. Thou bidst me go?
Give back the ship and comrade of my flight.
Why bid me go alone? Not so I came.
If thou fear war, both should go forth, nor choice
Be made between two equally at fault:
That old man fell for Jason's sake; impute

To Jason flight, rapine, a brother slain,
And a deserted father; not all mine
The crimes to which a husband tempted me;
'Tis true I sinned, but never for myself.

Creon. Thou shouldst begone, why waste the time with words?

Medea. I go, but going make one last request:
Let not a mother's guilt drag down her sons.

Creon. Go, as a father I will succor them,
And with a father's care.

Medea. By future hopes,
By the king's happy marriage, by the strength
Of thrones, which fickle fortune sometimes shakes,
I pray thee grant the exile some delay
That she, perchance about to die, may press
A last kiss on her children's lips.

Creon. Thou seekst
Time to commit new crime.

Medea. In so brief time
What crime were possible?

Creon. No time too short
For him who would do ill.

Medea. Dost thou deny
To misery short space for tears?

Creon. Deep dread
Warns me against thy prayer; yet I will grant
One day in which thou mayst prepare for flight.

Medea. Too great the favor! Of the time allowed,
Something withdraw. I would depart in haste.

Creon. Before the coming day is ushered in
By Phœbus, leave the city or thou diest.

The bridal calls me, and I go to pay
My vows to Hymen.

Scene III

Chorus. He rashly ventured who was first to make
In his frail boat a pathway through the deep;
Who saw his native land behind him fade
In distance blue; who to the raging winds
Trusted his life, his slender keel between
The paths of life and death. Our fathers dwelt
In an unspotted age, and on the shore
Where each was born he lived in quietness,
Grew old upon his father's farm content;
With little rich, he knew no other wealth
Than his own land afforded. None knew yet
The changing constellations, nor could use
As guides the stars that paint the ether; none
Had learned to shun the rainy Hyades,
The Goat, or Northern Wain, that follows slow
By old Boötes driven; none had yet
To Boreas or Zephyr given names.
Rash Tiphys was the first to tempt the deep
With spreading canvas; for the winds to write
New laws; to furl the sail; or spread it wide
When sailors longed to fly before the gale,
And the red topsail fluttered in the breeze.
The world so wisely severed by the seas
The pine of Thessaly united, bade
The distant waters bring us unknown fears.
The cursed leader paid hard penalty
When the two cliffs, the gateway of the sea,
Moved as though smitten by the thunderbolt,
And the imprisoned waters smote the stars.
Bold Tiphys paled, and from his trembling hand
Let fall the rudder; Orpheus' music died,
His lyre untouched; the Argo lost her voice.
When, belted by her girdle of wild dogs,
The maid of the Sicilian straits gives voice

From all her mouths, who fears not at her bark?
Who does not tremble at the witching song
With which the Sirens calm the Ausonian sea?
The Thracian Orpheus' lyre had almost forced
Those hinderers of ships to follow him!
What was the journey's prize? The golden fleece,
Medea, fiercer than the raging sea,—
Worthy reward for those first mariners!
The sea forgets its former wrath; submits
To the new laws; and not alone the ship
Minerva builded, manned by sons of kings,
Finds rowers; other ships may sail the deep.
Old metes are moved, new city walls spring up
On distant soil, and nothing now remains
As it has been. The cold Araxes' stream
The Indian drinks; the Persian quaffs the Rhine;
And the times come with the slow-rolling years
When ocean shall strike off the chains from earth,
And a great world be opened. Tiphys then,
Another Tiphys, shall win other lands,
And Thule cease to be earth's utmost bound.

ACT III

Scene I

Medea, Nurse.

Nurse. Stay, foster-child, why fly so swiftly hence?
Restrain thy wrath! curb thy impetuous haste!
As a Bacchante, frantic with the god
And filled with rage divine, uncertain walks
The top of snowy Pindus or the peak
Of Nyssa, so Medea wildly goes
Hither and thither; on her cheek the stain
Of bitter tears, her visage flushed, her breast
Shaken by sobs. She cries aloud, her eyes
Are drowned in scalding tears; again she laughs;
All passions surge within her soul; she stays
Her steps, she threatens, makes complaint, weeps, groans.
Where will she fling the burden of her soul?
Where wreak her vengeance? where will break this wave
Of fury? Passion overflows! she plans
No easy crime, no ordinary deed.
She conquers self; I recognize old signs
Of raging; something terrible she plans,
Some deed inhuman, devilish, and wild.
Ye gods, avert the horrors I foresee!

Medea. Dost thou seek how to show thy hate, poor wretch?
Imitate love! And must I then endure
Without revenge the royal marriage-torch?
Shall this day prove unfruitful, sought and gained
Only by earnest effort? While the earth
Hangs free within the heavens; while the vault
Of heaven sweeps round the earth with changeless change;
While the sands lie unnumbered; while the day
Follows the sun, the night brings up the stars;
Arcturus never wet in ocean's wave

Rolls round the pole; while rivers seaward flow,
My hate shall never cease to seek revenge.
Did ever fierceness of a ravening beast;
Or Scylla or Charybdis sucking down
The waters of the wild Ausonian
And the Sicilian seas; or Ætna fierce,
That holds imprisoned great Enceladus
Breathing forth flame, so glow as I with threats?
Not the swift rivers, nor the force of flame
By storm-wind fanned, can imitate my wrath.
I will o'erthrow and bring to naught the world!
Does Jason fear the king? Thessalian war?
True love fears nothing. He was forced to yield,
Unwillingly he gave his hand. But still
He might have sought his wife for one farewell.
This too he feared to do. He might have gained
From Creon some delay of banishment.
One day is granted for my two sons' sake!
I do not make complaint of too short time,
It is enough for much; this day shall see
What none shall ever hide. I will attack
The very gods, and shake the universe!

Nurse. Lady, thy spirit so disturbed by ills
Restrain, and let thy storm-tossed soul find rest.

Medea. Rest I can never find until I see
All dragged with me to ruin; all shall fall
When I do;—so to share one's woe is joy.

Nurse. Think what thou hast to fear if thou persist;
No one can safely fight with princely power.

Scene II

The Nurse withdraws; enter Jason.

Jason. The lot is ever hard; bitter is fate,
Equally bitter if it slay or spare;

22

God gives us remedies worse than our ills.
Would I keep faith with her I deem my wife
I must expect to die; would I shun death
I must forswear myself. Not fear of death
Has conquered honor, love has cast out fear
In that the father's death involves the sons.
O holy Justice, if thou dwell in heaven,
I call on thee to witness that the sons
Vanquish their father! Say the mother's love
Is fierce and spurns the yoke, she still will deem
Her children of more worth than marriage joys.
My mind is fixed, I go to her with prayers.
She starts at sight of me, her look grows wild,
Hatred she shows and grief.

Medea. Jason, I flee!
I flee, it is not new to change my home,
The cause of banishment alone is new;
I have been exiled hitherto for thee.
I go, as thou compellst me, from thy home,
But whither shall I go? Shall I, perhaps,
Seek Phasis, Colchis, and my father's realm
Whose soil is watered by a brother's blood?
What land dost thou command me seek? what sea?
The Euxine's jaws through which I led that band
Of noble princes when I followed thee,
Adulterer, through the Symplegades?
Little Iolchos? Tempe? Thessaly?
Whatever way I opened up for thee
I closed against myself. Where shall I go?
Thou drivest into exile, but hast given
No place of banishment. I will go hence.
The king, Creusa's father, bids me go,
And I will do his bidding. Heap on me
Most dreadful punishment, it is my due.
With cruel penalties let royal wrath
Pursue thy mistress, load my hands with chains,
And in a dungeon of eternal night
Imprison me—'tis less than I deserve!
Ungrateful one, recall the fiery bull;
The earth-born soldiers, who at my command

Slew one another; and the golden fleece
Of Phrixus' ram, whose watchful guardian,
The sleepless dragon, at my bidding slept;
The brother slain; the many, many crimes
In one crime gathered. Think how, led by me,
By me deceived, that old man's daughters dared
To slay their aged father, dead for aye!
By thy hearth's safety, by thy children's weal,
By the slain dragon, by these blood-stained hands
I never spared from doing aught for thee,
By thy past fears, and by the sea and sky
Witnesses of our marriage, pity me!
O happy one, give me some recompense!
Of all the ravished gold the Scythians brought
From far, as far as India's burning plains,
Wealth our wide palace hardly could contain,
So that we hung our groves with gold, I took
Nothing. My brother only bore I thence,
And him for thee I sacrificed. I left
My country, father, brother, maiden shame:
This was my marriage portion; give her own
To her who goes an exile.

Jason. When angry Creon thought to have thee slain,
Urged by my prayers, he gave thee banishment.

Medea. I looked for a reward; the gift I see
Is exile.

Jason. While thou mayst fly, fly in haste!
The wrath of kings is ever hard to bear.

Medea. Thou giv'st me such advice because thou lov'st
Creusa, wouldst divorce a hated wife!

Jason. And does Medea taunt me with my loves?

Medea. More—treacheries and murders.

Jason. Canst thou charge
Such sins to me?

Medea. All I have ever done.

Jason. It only needs that I should share the guilt
Of these thy crimes!

Medea. Thine are they, thine alone;
He is the criminal who reaps the fruit.
Though all should brand thy wife with infamy,
Thou shouldst defend and call her innocent:
She who has sinned for thee, toward thee is pure.

Jason. To me my life is an unwelcome gift
Of which I am ashamed.

Medea. Who is ashamed
To owe his life to me can lay it down.

Jason. For thy sons' sake control thy fiery heart.

Medea. I will have none of them, I cast them off,
Abjure them; shall Creusa to my sons
Give brothers?

Jason. To an exile's wretched sons
A mighty queen will give them.

Medea. Never come
That evil day that mingles a great race
With race unworthy,—Phœbus' glorious sons
With sons of Sisyphus.

Jason. What, cruel one,
Wouldst thou drag both to banishment? Away!

Medea. Creon has heard my prayer.

Jason. What can I do?

Medea. For me? Some crime perhaps.

Jason. A prince's wrath
Is here and there.

Medea. Medea's wrath more fierce!
Let us essay our power, the victor's prize
Be Jason.

Jason. Passion-weary, I depart;
Fear thou to trust a fate too often tried.

Medea. Fortune has ever served me faithfully.

Jason. Acastus comes.

Medea. Creon's a nearer foe,
But both shall fall. Medea does not ask
That thou shouldst arm thyself against the king,
Or soil thy hands with murder of thy kin;
Fly with me innocent.

Jason. Who will oppose
If double war ensue, and the two kings
Join forces?

Medea. Add to them the Colchian troops
And King Æëtes, Scythian hosts and Greeks,
Medea conquers them!

Jason. I greatly fear
A scepter's power.

Medea. Do not covet it.

Jason. We must cut short our converse, lest it breed
Suspicion.

Medea. Now from high Olympus send
Thy thunder, Jupiter; stretch forth thy hand,
Prepare thy lightning, from the riven clouds

Make the world tremble, nor with careful hand
Spare him or me; whichever of us dies
Dies guilty; thy avenging thunderbolt
Cannot mistake the victim.

Jason. Try to speak
More sanely; calm thyself. If aught can aid
Thy flight from Creon's house, thou needst but ask.

Medea. My soul is strong enough, and wont to scorn
The wealth of kings; this boon alone I crave,
To take my children with me when I go;
Into their bosoms I would shed my tears,
New sons are thine.

Jason. Would I might grant thy prayer;
Paternal love forbids me, Creon's self
Could not compel me to it. They alone
Lighten the sorrow of a grief-parched soul.
For them I live, I sooner would resign
Breath, members, light.

Medea [aside]. 'Tis well! He loves his sons,
This, then, the place where he may feel a wound!
[To Jason.] Before I go, thou wilt, at least, permit
That I should give my sons a last farewell,
A last embrace? But one thing more I ask:
If in my grief I've poured forth threatening words,
Retain them not in mind; let memory hold
Only my softer speech, my words of wrath
Obliterate.

Jason. I have erased them all
From my remembrance. I would counsel thee
Be calm, act gently; calmness quiets pain.

Exit Jason.

Scene III

Medea, Nurse.

Medea. He's gone! And can it be he leaves me so,
Forgetting me and all my guilt? Forgot?
Nay, never shall Medea be forgot!
Up! Act! Call all thy power to aid thee now;
This fruit of crime is thine, to shun no crime!
Deceit is useless, so they fear my guile.
Strike where they do not dream thou canst be feared.
Medea, haste, be bold to undertake
The possible—yea, that which is not so!
Thou, faithful nurse, companion of my griefs
And varying fortunes, aid my wretched plans.
I have a robe, gift of the heavenly powers,
An ornament of a king's palace, given
By Phœbus to my father as a pledge
Of sonship; and a necklace of wrought gold;
And a bright diadem, inlaid with gems,
With which they used to bind my hair. These gifts,
Endued with poison by my magic arts,
My sons shall carry for me to the bride.
Pay vows to Hecate, bring the sacrifice,
Set up the altars. Let the mounting flame
Envelop all the house.

Scene IV

Chorus. Fear not the power of flame, nor swelling gale,
Nor hurtling dart, nor cloudy wain that brings
The winter storms; fear not when Danube sweeps
Unchecked between its widely severed shores,
Nor when the Rhone hastes seaward, and the sun
Has broken up the snow upon the hills,
And Hermes flows in rivers.
A wife deserted, loving while she hates,
Fear greatly; blindly burns her anger's flame,

For kings she cares not, will not bear the curb.
Ye gods, we ask your grace divine for him
Who safely crossed the seas; the ocean's lord
Is angry for his conquered kingdom's sake;
Spare Jason, we entreat!
Th' impetuous youth who dared to drive the car
Of Phœbus, keeping not the wonted course,
Died in the furious fires himself had lit.
Few are the evils of the well-known way;
Seek the old paths your fathers safely trod,
The sacred federations of the world
Keep still inviolate.
The men who dipped the oars of that brave ship;
Who plundered of their shade the sacred groves
Of Pelion; passed between the unstable cliffs;
Endured so many hardships on the deep;
And cast their anchor on a savage coast,
Passing again with ravished foreign gold,
Atoned with fearful death upon the sea
For violated law.
The angry deep demanded punishment:
Tiphys to an unskillful pilot left
The rudder. On a foreign coast he fell,
Far from his father's kingdom, and he lies
With nameless shades, under a lowly tomb.
Becalmed in her still harbor Aulis held
The impatient ships, remembering in wrath
The king that she lost thence.
The fair Camena's son, who touched his lyre
So sweetly that the floods stood still, the winds
Were silent, and the birds forgot to sing,
And forests followed him, on Thracian fields
Lies dead, his head borne down by Hebrus' stream.
He touched again the Styx and Tartarus,
But not again returns.
Alcides overthrew the north wind's sons;
He slew that son of Neptune who could take
Unnumbered forms; but after he had made
Peace between land and sea, and opened wide
The realm of Dis, lying on Œta's top
He gave his body to the cruel fire,

Destroyed by his wife's gift—the fatal robe
Poisoned with Centaur's blood.
Ankæus fell a victim to the boar
Of Caledonia; Meleager slew
His mother's brother, stained his hands with blood
Of his own mother. They have merited
Their lot, but what the crime that he atoned
By death whom Hercules long sought in vain—
The tender Hylas drawn beneath safe waves?
Go now, brave soldiers, boldly plow the main,
But fear the gentle streams.
Idmon the serpents buried in the sands
Of Libya, though he knew the future well.
Mopsus, to others true, false to himself,
Fell far from Thebes; and he who tried to burn
The crafty Greeks fell headlong to the deep:
Such death was meet for crime.
Oileus, smitten by the thunderbolt,
Died on the ocean; and Pheræus' wife
Fell for her husband, so averting fate;
He who commanded that the golden spoil
Be carried to the ships had traveled far,
But, plunged in seething cauldron, Pelias died
In narrow limits. 'Tis enough, ye gods;
Ye have avenged the sea!

ACT IV

Scene I

Nurse. I shrink with horror! Ruin threatens us!
How terribly her wrath inflames itself!
Her former force awakes, thus I have seen
Medea raging and attacking god,
Compelling heaven. Greater crime than then
She now prepares, for as with frantic step
She sought the sanctuary of her crimes,
She poured forth all her threats; and what before
She feared she now brings forth; lets loose a host
Of poisonous evils, arts mysterious;
With sad left hand outstretched invokes all ills
That Libyan sands with their fierce heat create,
Or frost-bound Taurus with perpetual snow
Encompasses. Drawn by her magic spell
The serpent drags his heavy length along,
Darts his forked tongue, and seeks his destined prey.
Hearing her incantation, he draws back
And knots his swelling body coiling it.—
'They are but feeble poisons earth brings forth,
And harmless darts,' she says, 'heaven's ills I seek.
Now is the time for deeper sorcery.
The dragon like a torrent shall descend,
Whose mighty folds the Great and Lesser Bear
Know well; Ophiuchus shall loose his grasp
And poison flow. Be present at my call,
Python, who dared to fight twin deities.
The Hydra slain by Hercules shall come
Healed of his wound. Thou watchful Colchian one,
Be present with the rest—thou, who first slept
Lulled by my incantations.' When the brood
Of serpents has been called she blends the juice
Of poisonous herbs; all Eryx' pathless heights

Bear, or the open top of Caucasus
Wet with Prometheus' blood, where winter reigns;
All that the rich Arabians use to tip
Their poisoned shafts, or the light Parthians,
Or warlike Medes; all the brave Suabians cull
In the Hyrcanian forests in the north;
All poisons that the earth brings forth in spring
When birds are nesting; or when winter cold
Has torn away the beauty of the groves
And bound the world in icy manacles.
Whatever herb gives flower the cause of death,
Or juice of twisted root, her hands have culled.
These on Thessalian Athos grew, and those
On mighty Pindus; on Pangæus' height
She cut the tender herbs with bloody scythe.
These Tigris nurtured with its current deep,
The Danube those; Hydaspes rich in gems
Flowing with current warm through levels dry,
Bætis that gives its name to neighboring lands
And meets the western ocean languidly,
Have nurtured these. Those have been cut at dawn;
These other herbs at dead of night were reaped;
And these were gathered with the enchanted hook.
Death-dealing plants she chooses, wrings the blood
Of serpents, and she takes ill-omened birds,
The sad owl's heart, the quivering entrails cut
From the horned owl living;—sorts all these.
In some the eager force of flame is found,
In some the bitter cold of sluggish ice;
To these she adds the venom of her words
As greatly to be feared. She stamps her feet;
She sings, and the world trembles at her song.

Scene II

Medea, before the altar of Hecate.
Medea. Here I invoke you, silent company,
Infernal gods, blind Chaos, sunless home
Of shadowy Dis, and squalid caves of Death
Bound by the banks of Tartarus. Lost souls,

For this new bridal leave your wonted toil.
Stand still, thou whirling wheel, Ixion touch
Again firm ground; come, Tantalus, and drink
Unchecked the wave of the Pirenian fount.
Let heavier punishment on Creon wait:—
Thou stone of Sisyphus, worn smooth, roll back;
And ye Danaïdes who strive in vain
To fill your leaking jars, I need your aid.
Come at my invocation, star of night,
Endued with form most horrible, nor threat
With single face, thou three-formed deity!
To thee, according to my country's use,
With hair unfilleted and naked feet
I've trod the sacred groves; called forth the rain
From cloudless skies; have driven back the sea;
And forced the ocean to withdraw its waves.
Earth sees heaven's laws confused, the sun and stars
Shining together, and the two Bears wet
In the forbidden ocean. I have changed
The circle of the seasons:—at my word
Earth flourishes with summer; Ceres sees
A winter harvest; Phasis' rushing stream
Flows to its source; the Danube that divides
Into so many mouths restrains its flood
Of waters—hardly moving past its shores.
The winds are silent; but the waters speak,
The wild seas roar; the home of ancient groves
Loses its leafy shade; the day withdraws
At my command; the sun stands still in heaven.
My incantations move the Hyades.
It is thy hour, Diana!
For thee my bloody hands have wrought this crown
Nine times by serpents girt; those knotted snakes
Rebellious Typhon bore, who made revolt
Against Jove's kingdom; Nessus gave this blood
When dying; Œta's funeral pyre provides
These ashes which have drunk the poisoned blood
Of dying Hercules; and here thou seest
Althea's vengeful brand. The harpies left
These feathers in the pathless den they made
A refuge when they fled from Zete's wrath;

And these were dropped by the Stymphalian birds
That felt the wound of arrows dipped in blood
Of the Lernæan Hydra.
The altars find a voice, the tripod moves
Stirred by the favoring goddess. Her swift car
I see approach—not the full-orbed that rolls
All night through heaven; but as, with darkened light,
Troubled by the Thessalians she comes,
So her sad face upon my altars sheds
A murky light. Terrify with new dread
The men of earth! Costly Corinthian brass
Sounds in thy honor, Hecate, and on ground
Made red with blood I pay these solemn rites
To thee; for thee have stolen from the tomb
This torch that gives its baleful funeral light;
To thee with bowed head I have made my prayer;
And in accordance with my country's use,
My loose hair filleted, have plucked for thee
This branch that grows beside the Stygian wave;
Like a wild Mænad, laying bare my breast,
With sacred knife I cut for thee my arm;
My blood is on the altars! Hand, learn well
To strike thy dearest! See, my blood flows forth!
Daughter of Perseus, have I asked too oft
Thine aid? Recall no more my former prayers.
To-day as always I invoke thine aid
For Jason's sake alone! Endue this robe
With such a baleful power that the bride
May feel at its first touch consuming fire
Of serpent's poison in her inmost veins;
Let fire lurk hid in the bright gold, the fire
Prometheus gave and taught men how to store—
He now atones his daring theft from heaven
With tortured vitals. Mulciber has given
This flame, and I in sulphur nurtured it;
I brought a spark from the destroying fire
Of Phaeton; I have the flame breathed forth
By the Chimæra, and the fire I snatched
From Colchis' savage bull; and mixed with these
Medusa's venom. I have bade all serve
My secret sorcery; now, Hecate, add

The sting of poison, aid the seeds of flame
Hid in my gift; let them deceive the sight
But burn the touch; let the heat penetrate
Her very heart and veins, stiffen her limbs,
Consume her bones in smoke. Her burning hair
Shall glow more brightly than the nuptial torch!
My vows are paid, and Hecate thrice has barked,
And shaken fire from her funeral torch.
'Tis finished! Call my sons. My precious gifts,
Ye shall be borne by them to the new bride.
Go, go, my sons, a hapless mother's sons!
Placate with gifts and prayers your father's wife!
But come again with speed, that I may know
A last embrace!

Scene III

Chorus. Where hastes the blood-stained Maenad, headlong driven
By angry love? What mischief plots her rage?
With wrath her face grows rigid; her proud head
She fiercely shakes; threatens the king in wrath.
Who would believe her exiled from the realm?
Her cheeks glow crimson, pallor puts to flight
The red, no color lingers on her face;
Her steps are driven to and fro as when
A tiger rages, of its young bereft,
Beside the Ganges in the gloomy woods.
Medea knows not how to curb her love
Or hate. Now love and hate together rage.
When will she leave the fair Pelasgian fields,
The wicked Colchian one, and free from fear
Our king and kingdom? Drive with no slow rein
Thy car, Diana; let the sweet night hide
The sunlight. Hesperus, end the dreaded day.

ACT V

Scene I

Messenger, Chorus.

Messenger [enters in haste]. All are destroyed, the royal empire falls,
Father and child lie in one funeral pyre.

Chorus. Destroyed by what deceit?

Messenger. That which is wont
To ruin princes—gifts.

Chorus. Could these work harm?

Messenger. I myself wonder, and can hardly deem
The wrong accomplished, though I know it done.

Chorus. How did it happen?

Messenger. A destructive fire
Spreads everywhere as at command; even now
The city is in fear, the palace burned.

Chorus. Let water quench the flames.

Messenger. It will not these,
As by a miracle floods feed the fire.
The more we fight it so much more it glows.

Scene II

Medea, Nurse.

Nurse. Up! up! Medea! Swiftly flee the land

Of Pelops; seek in haste a distant shore.

Medea. Shall I fly? I? Were I already gone
I would return for this, that I might see
These new betrothals. Dost thou pause, my soul?
This joy's but the beginning of revenge.
Thou dost but love if thou art satisfied
To widow Jason. Seek new penalties,
Honor is gone and maiden modesty,—
It were a light revenge pure hands could yield.
Strengthen thy drooping spirit, stir up wrath,
Drain from thy heart its all of ancient force,
Thy deeds till now call honor; wake, and act,
That they may see how light, how little worth,
All former crime—the prelude of revenge!
What was there great my novice hands could dare?
What was the madness of my girlhood days?
I am Medea now, through sorrow strong.
Rejoice, because through thee thy brother died;
Rejoice, because through thee his limbs were torn,
Through thee thy father lost the golden fleece;
Rejoice, that armed by thee his daughters slew
Old Pelias! Seek revenge! No novice hand
Thou bring'st to crime; what wilt thou do; what dart
Let fly against thy hated enemy?
I know not what my maddened spirit plots,
Nor yet dare I confess it to myself!
In folly I made haste—would that my foe
Had children by this other! Mine are his,
We'll say Creusa bore them! 'Tis enough;
Through them my heart at last finds full revenge;
My soul must be prepared for this last crime.
Ye who were once my children, mine no more,
Ye pay the forfeit for your father's crimes.
Awe strikes my spirit and benumbs my hand;
My heart beats wildly; mother-love drives out
Hate of my husband; shall I shed their blood—
My children's blood? Demented one, rage not,
Be far from thee this crime! What guilt is theirs?
Is Jason not their father?—guilt enough!
And worse, Medea claims them as her sons.

They are not sons of mine, so let them die!
Nay, rather let them perish since they are!
But they are innocent—my brother was!
Fear'st thou? Do tears already mar thy cheek?
Do wrath and love like adverse tides impel
Now here, now there? As when the winds wage war,
And the wild waves against each other smite,
My heart is beaten; duty drives out fear,
As wrath drives duty. Anger dies in love.
Dear sons, sole solace of a storm-tossed house,
Come hither, he may have you safe if I
May claim you too! But he has banished me;
Already from my bosom torn away
They go lamenting—perish then to both,
To him as me! My wrath again grows hot;
Furies, I go wherever you may lead.
Would that the children of the haughty child
Of Tantalus were mine, that I had borne
Twice seven sons! In bearing only two
I have been cursed! And yet it is enough
For father, brother, that I have borne two.—
Where does that horde of furies haste? whom seek?
For whom prepare their fires? or for whom
Intends the infernal band its bloody torch?
Whom does Megaera seek with hostile brand?
The mighty dragon lashes its fierce tail—
What shade uncertain brings its scattered limbs?
It is my brother, and he seeks revenge;
I grant it, thrust the torches in my eyes;
Kill, burn, the furies have me in their power!
Brother, command the avenging goddesses
To leave me, and the shades to seek their place
In the infernal regions without fear;
Here leave me to myself, and use this hand
That held the sword—your soul has found revenge. [Kills one of her sons.
What is the sudden noise? They come in arms
And think to drive me into banishment.
I will go up on the high roof, come thou;
I'll take the body with me. Now my soul,
Strike! hold not hid thy power, but show the world
What thou art able.

She goes out with the nurse and the living boy, and carries with her the body of her dead son.

Scene III

Jason in the foreground, Medea with the children appears upon the roof.

Jason. Ye faithful ones, who share
In the misfortunes of your harassed king,
Hasten to take the author of these deeds.
Come hither, hither, cohorts of brave men;
Bring up your weapons; overthrow the house.

Medea. I have recaptured now my crown and throne,
My brother and my father; Colchians hold
The golden fleece; my kingdom is won back;
My lost virginity returns to me!
O gods appeased, marriage, and happy days,
Go now,—my vengeance is complete! Not yet—
Finish it while thy hands are strong to strike.
Why seek delay? Why hesitate, my soul?
Thou art able! All thine anger falls to nought!
I do repent of that which I have done!
Why did'st thou do it, miserable one?
Yea, miserable! Ruth shall follow thee!
'Tis done, great joy fills my unwilling heart,
And, lo, the joy increases But one thing
Before was lacking—Jason did not see!
All that he has not seen I count as lost.

Jason. She threatens from the roof; let fire be brought,
That she may perish burned with her own flame.

Medea. Pile high the funeral pyre of thy sons,
And rear their tomb. To Creon and thy wife
I have already paid the honors due.
This son is dead, and this shall soon be so,
And thou shalt see him perish.

Jason. By the gods,
By our sad flight together, and the bond
I have not willingly forsaken, spare
Our son! If there is any crime, 'tis mine;
Put me to death, strike down the guilty one.

Medea. There where thou askest mercy, and canst feel
The sting, I thrust the sword. Go, Jason, seek
Thy virgin bride, desert a mother's bed.

Jason. Let one suffice for vengeance.

Medea. Had it been
That one could satisfy my hands with blood,
I had slain none. But two is not enough.

Jason. Then go, fill up the measure of thy crime,
I ask for nothing but that thou should'st make
A speedy end.

Medea. Now, grief, take slow revenge;
It is my day; haste not, let me enjoy.

[Kills the other child.]

Jason. Slay me, mine enemy!

Medea. Dost thou implore
My pity? It is well! I am avenged.
Grief, there is nothing more that thou canst slay!
Look up, ungrateful Jason, recognize
Thy wife; so I am wont to flee. The way
Lies open through the skies; two dragons bend
Their necks, submissive to the yoke. I go
In my bright car through heaven. Take thy sons!

She casts down to him the bodies of her children, and is borne away in a chariot drawn by dragons.

Jason. Go through the skies sublime, and going prove
That the gods dwell not in the heavens you seek.

THE END

Made in the USA
Coppell, TX
09 November 2020